# Sergi Arola

## Cooking Is Fun

Photographs by Ángel Becerril
Translation by Spencer Groves

SALSA

BARCELONA

S A L S A

B O O K S

First Edition: May 2004.
© Text: Sergi Arola, 2004.
© Photographs, including the back cover: Ángel Becerril, 2004.
© Prologue: Juan Manuel Bellver, 2004.
© Translation: Spencer Groves, 2004.
© This edition: Edicions 62
Peu de la Creu 4, 08001 Barcelona
correu@grup62.com
grup62.com

Typesetting and dust jacket by Malaidea
Filmsetting by Víctor Igual
Printed by Grafos
Legal Deposit: 23.528-2004
ISBN: 84-297-5483-0

# Contents

Manchego Cheese and Olive Oil Ice Cream \
Potato Confit with Salt Cod Brandade and
Black Truffles

Sweet Sugar
  Carrots with Yoghurt, Pistachios and Cumin \
  White Chocolate Brownie with Caramelized
  Apple, Afuega'l Pitu Cream and Crème Caramel
  Ice Cream \ Super Macaroon Cookies \ Peach
  Confit with Amaretto and Leek Crunchies \
  Orange Sponge with Crème Caramel Ice Cream
  and Turron Foam \ Bread with Chocolate and
  Sugar \ Fennel Sorbet and Apple Gelatine \
  Chestnuts and French Toast with Lemon Ice
  Cream and Orange and Cinnamon Foam \
  Bread with Oil, Sugar and Lime \ Breadsticks
  with Three Sauces

      Step by Step
      Parsley Oil \ Lemon Infusion \ Green Pepper
      Gelatine (Agar-Agar) \ Soy Sauce Gelatine \ Hot
      Bacon Foam \ Bread Foam \ Sardines \ Ice
      Cream Base

          Glossary of Material
          Technical Vocabulary

# Cooking
## in the pop era

Modern Spanish cuisine is fashionable all over the world. For a few years, the enthusiastic work of about twenty, or perhaps thirty, young chefs has shattered all the preconceptions about the country's top-class catering business, and it is now being recognised worldwide and even imitated. The formula for their success is based on a thorough research into the possibilities of new technologies and on a conception of culinary creativity that is rooted and respectful towards the product, while fiercely liberated from long standing affectations. It is vocationally happy, delicious, light, colourful, participative, sometimes impressive or dramatic, usually charming, whether you delve into its coherent intellectual framework or you enjoy it frivolously through your senses and emotions. If we had to approach this phenomenon from the point of view of an art or music critic, we would define it as intelligent pop.

Sergi Arola forms part of that elite of artistic chefs that have instilled their culinary wisdom into the top restaurants of the Iberian peninsula. But he, due to the vagaries of fate, ended up with perhaps the most difficult role in this quiet revolution: triumphing in Madrid. The Spanish capital, as a political and economic centre, a metropolis based on the service sector that is sick of business lunches and appearances, urban stress and intensive relationships, a dreary market for whoever expects the diner to leisurely dedicate two hours to the social formalities of eating out and focus his or her attention on the plate all the way through the meal.

Sergi arrived at the Spanish capital in 1997,
coming directly from his native Barcelona,
with the guarantee of having worked side by
side with the master Ferran Adrià. He came to
regenerate a tiny bistro in Chamartín, officiating
from a kitchen of only eight square metres. And
the rest is history: his culinary style, never
before seen in the city, sparked an instant
following from critics and the general public
alike, surpassing all expectations and rewarding
him with the highest ratings in guidebooks and
numerous prizes. The move to his current
location, an independent, light and minimalist
kitchen in the Occidental Miguel Ángel Hotel,
took place in the year 2000. And he has
continued receiving honours, including, so far,
his two Michelin stars and the National
Gastronomy Prize.

Sergi has earned his reputation from scratch:
from his first youthful vocation as a bassist in a
rock band to his retraining as a professional
cook, including his courage to change city and
come to preach to a one-horse town in La
Mancha that is constantly bustling. Anybody
else would have slipped up on the way, but he
has additional talents (a work ethic, the ability
to adapt and get on well with people) that are
additional to his skills in the kitchen: not only
was he the first person to bring the concepts
from the highly innovative Catalan cuisine to
Madrid, but after captivating the residents and
becoming –without expecting it– the most
prestigious chef in the city, he also knew how to
sensibly adapt his desire to experiment to his
customers' palate, calming his culinary
repertoire until reaching a very personal style
that he himself defines as "twenty-first century
bourgeois creative cuisine" or something of the
sort (it could also be "urban cuisine for modern
people", but who cares about labels).

The intelligent evolution that has taken place
in these last few years is reflected in this

present volume of recipes. There is no need for any additions or unnecessary explanations. Of course, there are a couple of previous books (*Dos horas con Sergi Arola*, by Jaume Coll, and *Como quieras, cuando quieras, donde quieras: en la cocina de Sergi Arola*, with texts by David Trueba) that also offer some of our man's dishes. To all who already have them, *Cooking Is Fun* is an essential complement, since it contributes forty new creations from the chef at his professional peak, with a tone of studied simplicity and a search for well-defined flavours and combinations whose effectiveness has been proved (not in vain – all the recipes compiled in this book were a hit in La Broche during recent years). To all those who approach Sergi's culinary universe for the first time, you will find here, divided into three sections ("Mountain and Coastal Cuisine", "From the Imagination" and "Sweet Sugar"), many of the keys that define his personal perspective on cooking: it is daring and light, evocative and genuine, witty, geometric and with a very catchy, hedonistic attitude.

All the recipes are explained with simplicity and photographed without pretence, while offering alternative versions for home use that can solve the lack of this or that ingredient or utensil. Face up to them without making a fuss or too much solemnity, because they have been written only with the aim of tantalizing the taste buds and reaching the heart through the senses. I ike the glorious chorus of a classic pop song.

Juan Manuel Bellver
April 2004

# Cooking can be
# fun… or not

It is true, cooking can be fun… or not, or at
least that is the conclusion that one arrives
at when, having published a recipe in any
magazine, one receives the congratulations
accompanied by the criticism, or the criticism
accompanied by the congratulations —it
amounts to the same thing— from those who,
inspired by a culinary passion, tried to follow
it for a family gathering or a dinner party
with colleagues from the office…

It is also true that, as in so many other
aspects of the fine arts, when one creates a
recipe one tries to show the restaurant-
going public a personal conception of taste,
a way to understand and combine flavours,
a way to express one's aesthetic values… in
short, to try to show the diner how one
understands and lives one's profession.

The widespread and popular belief that us
chefs tend not to reveal all our cards is —on
my word of honour— if not false then quite
wide of the mark. Look at it from this
perspective: in a restaurant such as La
Broche, with a team of never less than
fifteen people in the kitchen, all of them
professionals eager to constantly improve
and working at least twelve hours a day…
you will understand that neither secrets nor
half-truths in the recipes are necessary,
since in the end our infallible secret is none
other than hard work and the outmost
concentration of what is in my opinion the
best team of chefs in the world…

Regardless of this, as a recipe book is something altogether different and my sincere intention is for you to enjoy these forty recipes that I offer you, some of them distinctly modern and some that have been around for a while. As well as offering every recipe accompanied by a strictly neutral photograph, without conditioning any type of crockery or accessories, we add certain tips that have occurred to us to make the recipes simpler, without "castrating" or distorting the original version. In other words, if one has all the necessary gadgets at home (Pacojet, Thermomix, Siphon, etc.) one ought to be capable, with a certain amount of patience and technique, of following the recipe just as we do in La Broche. If you do not want too many complications, you can use the alternative ingredients that we propose at the end; we guarantee that our only desire is to open a window onto new or at least not so commonly encountered combinations. I hope that with this we are able to awaken in you the bug for modern cuisine with the chef's personal stamp and for trying out not only our restaurant, which is also yours, but also every one of those hundreds of establishments run by young people who day after day are contributing to making gastronomy something alive and dynamic, putting all their illusions and best efforts, and following in the footsteps of the great master chefs. We are working every day to carry on making Spanish gastronomy "by rights" —as my friends from Cadiz say— one of the most prestigious in the world.

# Mountain and Coastal Cuisine

## Ingredients:

**For the platter:**
60 g lobster \ 20 g clams \ 10 g cockles \ 50 g king prawns \ 10 g goose barnacles \ 25 g mussels \ 30 g sea bass \ 50 g scorpion fish

**For the soup:**
1 lobster head \ 100 g frozen king prawns \ 1 red onion \ 3 cloves of garlic \ 1 tablespoon paprika \ 200 ml Pernod

**For the saffron agar:**
50 ml water \ 1 thin slice of garlic \ a few saffron threads \ 0.3 g agar-agar per litre

**For the king prawn agar:**
1 king prawn head \ 50 ml water \ 0.3 g agar-agar per litre

**For the "picada":**
10 g fried hazelnuts \ 10 g fried almonds \ 10 fried bread \ 20 fried parsley leaves \ 100 ml olive oil (0.4° acidity) for frying

**For the crisps:**
2 cloves of garlic \ 1 slice of sliced white bread \ 1 ripe tomato \ 8 parsley leaves

## Preparation:

**1. For the platter:**
Blanch the molluscs, rinse and reserve in a cool place. Clean the fish and cut it into portions. Cut the lobster into medallions. Just before serving, sear them on the griddle and finish off in the oven or in a Salamander.

**2. For the soup:**
Chop the onions and soften them slowly. Add the paprika and Pernod and reduce. Add the lobster head and reduce to half the volume, and then strain.

**3. For the saffron agar:**
Sauté the garlic and place it with the lightly toasted saffron in the water, bring to the boil and crush. Allow to cool and strain. Pour into a sauce bottle and keep cool. Add the agar-agar, bring to the boil and allow to set. Mash in the Thermomix and strain.

# Warm Lobster Soup with Coastal Fish and Molluscs

### 4. For the king prawn agar:

Sauté the prawn heads, add the water and cook for 20 minutes. Crush and strain. Add the agar-agar, bring to the boil and allow to set. Mash in the Thermomix, strain and transfer to a sauce bottle.

### 5. For the "picada":

Fry all the ingredients. Mash them in the Thermomix, along with the cooled oil used for frying.

### 6. For the crisps:

Fry the sliced garlic in a little olive oil, adding it while the oil is still cold. Fry the parsley leaves. Cut the bread into small squares and fry. Slice the tomato finely, taking care to keep whole pieces and dry in a food dehydrator.

## Presentation:

Sear all the molluscs on one side of the griddle and seal the skin of the pieces of fish. Place them around the plate, and alternate drops of the saffron emulsion and the king prawn emulsion. Finish off by adding the "picada" and parsley crisps, garlic crisps and mini pieces of toast.

## Ingredients:

4 large crayfish \ 10 ml ginger infused oil \ 10 ml garlic infused oil \ 1 aubergine \ 10 ml teriyaki \ 10 ml soy sauce \ 10 ml honey \ 30 g rocket \ 2 g salt \ 10 ml extra virgin olive oil \ 24 ml base syrup (12 g sugar in 12 ml water) \ 5 ml dashi \ 100 ml olive oil \ 1 lemon \ a few drops of sherry vinegar

## Preparation:

### 1. For the crayfish:

Remove the shells of the crayfish and keep the heads and claws. Thread the crayfish onto a brochette. Just before serving, sear on a high flame in a non-stick frying pan in 0.4° acidity olive oil and salt. Sauté the heads with the lightest possible 0.4° acidity olive oil and press into a colander to obtain the maximum juice possible from them. This sauce is known as an "essence" and is mixed with a little ginger oil.

2. Cut 4 very fine slices from the aubergine with the mandolin and allow them to dry in the oven at 100° C for an hour. When they have dried, coat them in the syrup and caramelize in the oven at 150° C for 10 minutes. Keep in a dry place on kitchen paper.

Cut the rest of the aubergine into a brunoise and sauté in garlic infused oil on a high heat, taking care that is does not burn. Remove the aubergine, and using the same pan, caramelize the honey. Add the teriyaki and the soy sauce, reduce to a fifth of its volume and return the aubergine to the pan.

3. Wash the rocket and reserve in iced water. Prepare the lemon vinaigrette by emulsifying the oil with the juice of half a lemon and adding a few drops of vinegar and salt.

# Crayfish with Aubergine Ratatouille and Rocket

## Presentation:

Place the aubergine ratatouille on the plate, and put the sautéed crayfish on top. Place the rocket dressed with the crayfish essence and lemon vinaigrette on one side, and on the other the aubergine crunchie.

## Ingredients:

4 fat razor clams \ 4 slices of country-style loaf \ 1 vine tomato \ 1 clove of garlic \ olive oil \ 4 thin slices of streaky bacon \ 4 sprigs of dill to garnish

### For the double cream:

500 ml cream \ 6 dried bay leaves \ 3 egg yolks \ salt and white pepper

## Preparation:

1. Based on the idea of the traditional "montaditos", this little open sandwich could not be easier to make. Cut the bread and toast the slices. Smear them lightly with a clove of garlic, rub in the juices of an opened tomato, splash with a little olive oil and sprinkle with salt. Next, dip the clams in boiling water for 5 seconds, wash and remove from their shells. Place on the pieces of toast in the form of a fan. Dry the bacon in the oven between two pieces of baking paper with a weight on top until they are crunchy. Reserve between two pieces of kitchen roll.

2. For the double cream:

Infuse the cream with the bay leaves for 10 minutes, and then add the egg yolks, salt and pepper to taste and cook in the Thermomix for 4.5 minutes at 80° C. Strain and allow to cool.

## Presentation:

Cover the clams on toast with the double cream and heat under the grill or in a Salamander. Garnish with a sprig of dill and a slice of crispy bacon.

# "Montadito" of Razor Clams with Double Cream of Bay and Streaky Bacon

## Ingredients:

4 cubes of desalted salt cod (each approx. 1 cm$^3$) \ olive oil \ parsley \ salt and white pepper

### For the red pepper gelatine:

400 g peeled red peppers \ 300 ml concentrated stock \ 1/2 jar "choricero" pepper flesh \ 3 g agar-agar \ 3 sheets of gelatine (each 2 g) \ salt and pepper

### For the aioli:

3 egg yolks \ oil of garlic infused oil \ Salt and pepper

## Preparation:

1. Roast the red peppers in the oven in a little oil at 180º C for 25 minutes and then peel.
2. Mash the roasted pepper and the "choricero" pepper flesh with the broth. Add the agar-agar and bring to the boil, and then add the sheets of gelatine. Strain and transfer 0.5 cm to each glass.
3. To obtain the parsley oil, blanch the parsley and crush it with a little oil, strain and reserve.
4. Finally, prepare the aioli sauce with the egg yolks and the garlic oil.

## Presentation:

Confit the cod in rosemary and thyme infused olive oil at 70º C, and then cover it with aioli and glaze in the Salamander. Pour the parsley oil into a circle in the glasses and place the grilled cod in the centre.

# Cod,
# Barcelona Style

# Ingredients for 4 people:

50 g smoked tuna \ 250 g ripe vine tomatoes \
1 sheet of gelatine \ 4 fresh oregano leaves \
45 ml cream \ 12 ml milk \ 50 g mozzarella
cheese \ anchovy salt \ extra virgin olive oil \
black pepper crystals

## Preparation:

1. Cut the tuna into 2 cm strips.

2. Smash the tomatoes, strain the pulp and
pass it through an etamine to obtain the
tomato juice. Dissolve the gelatine in 1/4 litre
of the tomato juice and season.

3. Mix the milk, the cream and the mozzarella
together. Heat until they dissolve, add salt,
pepper and stabilizer and allow to rest for 24
hours, and then freeze or place in the sorbet
maker.

4. To obtain the anchovy salt, leave the salt
that surrounds the anchovies to dry, and then
crush.

5. To obtain the pepper crystals, dilute the
sugar in water on low heat until it becomes a
clear caramel. Spread the caramel onto a
piece of greaseproof paper and sprinkle with
black pepper, cover with another piece of
paper and flatten with a rolling pin. Leave to
cool and break into pieces with your hands.

## Presentation:

Pile the tuna strips so they form a tower, and
place the mozzarella ice cream on top,
followed by a splash of olive oil, an oregano
leaf, the pepper crystals and the tomato
soup. Sprinkle with the anchovy salt.

# Smoked Tuna with Tomato Soup and Mozzarella Ice Cream

Note: You can substitute the mozzarella ice
cream with a piece of good quality
mozzarella or fresh cheese ice cream from
an ice cream parlour.

## Ingredients:

Granny Smith apples \ fresh chilli pepper cut in a very thin julienne \ Maldon sea salt and ground black pepper \ 12 anchovies \ 3 gherkins in vinegar

### For the apple vinaigrette:

2 l cider, reduced to 1/4 l \ 100 g sugar \ 50 g cider vinegar \ 100 ml Hojiblanca olive oil (0.4° acidity) \ 10 ml egg white \ 1 clove of garlic

### For the cider caramel:

100 g sugar \ 1 l cider vinegar

## Preparation:

1. Scale and gut the anchovies, removing the heads. Open them up and bone, leaving the two fillets joined together. Place one anchovy with the skin side down on top of a slice of gherkin of the same length. Place another anchovy on top with the skin side facing upwards. Cut the top anchovy into four pieces.

2. Cut the apple into cubes. If it is not used immediately, cover with water and lemon.

3. The vinaigrette is made by emulsifying the reduced cider with the egg white, sugar, vinegar and the olive oil. Add salt, strain and transfer to a sauce bottle.

4. Reduce the vinegar with the sugar until obtaining a thin syrup caramel.

5. Slice the garlic and fry in a little olive oil, adding the garlic while the oil is still cold.

## Presentation:

Place the pieces of apple in a line at the top of a small square plate. Place the slices of gherkin perpendicular to the apple, and on top of these the anchovies, after cooking them in the Salamander with a little oil and salt. Draw a square with the cider caramel and season the cubes of apple with a little emulsion. Place the ginger and the garlic

# Butterflied Anchovies with Pickles and Apple Salad

chips over the anchovies, along with a sprig of chervil. Finish off with a grind of the pepper mill.

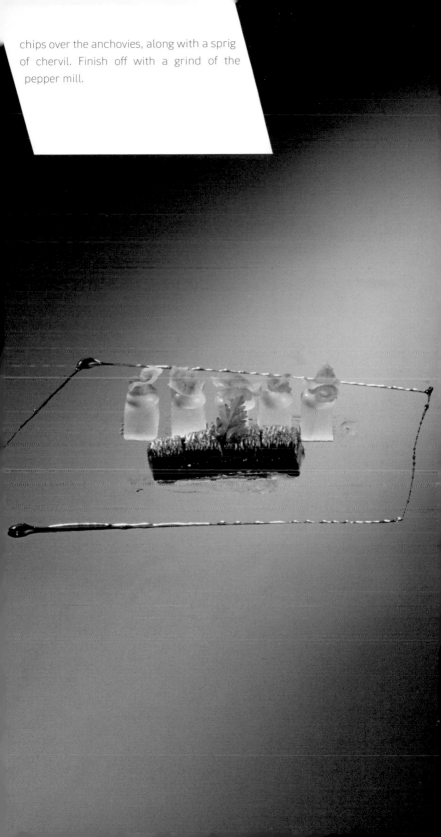

## Ingredients:

30 g Kenyan green beans \ 30 g black chanterelle mushrooms \ 15 g sobrasada sausage \ 40 ml olive oil (0.4° acidity) \ 150 g sardines \ 50 ml aged Cabernet Sauvignon vinegar \ 2.5 g sugar \ 1 g Maldon sea salt \ 5 g chives

### Preparation:

#### 1. For the green beans:

Wash and cut into equal sized pieces. Blanch in boiling water for 1 minute and refresh with iced water. Just before serving, sauté on a high heat for 3 minutes.

#### 2. For the mushrooms:

Wipe off all the earth with a damp cloth and cut off the base of the stems. Sauté just before serving on a high heat for 3 minutes.

#### 3. For the sobrasada:

Cut into small cubes and confit the pieces in 0.4° acidity olive oil for half an hour on a low heat. Strain and reserve. Sauté the sobrassada. Reduce the vinegar with the sugar for approximately one hour until is turns to syrup. Cut the chives into small pieces.

#### 4. For the sardines:

Clean and scale the sardines, remove the loin and sear the skin side in a frying pan. Finish cooking in a hot oven.

# Roast Sardines with Black Chanterelle Mushrooms, Kenyan Green Beans and Sobrasada

### Presentation:

Pile the green beans and the black chanterelle mushrooms in the centre of the plate, on top of the sardines. Place the sobrasada around them, along with the sobrasada oil and on top of them the vinegar reduction. Sprinkle the chopped chives over the top.

## Ingredients:

1 fleshy green pepper \ 1 red pepper \ 4 baby aubergines \ 4 shallots or baby onions \ 1 new potato \ 100 g chicken gizzards confited in their own fat \ 100 g cock's combs confited in their own fat \ 1 clove of garlic from Las Pedroñeras \ 1 purple onion \ 1 l concentrated chicken stock \ 50 g peeled sunflower seeds \ 200 ml sunflower oil \ salt and pepper \ 50 g parmesan cheese, grated

## Preparation:

1. Make a rillette by finely chopping the garlic, onion, chicken gizzards and cock's combs and lightly frying everything until it browns. Drain all the fat away and add a little stock. Mix everything together in a blender until it is an even mass and allow to cool.

2. Roast the vegetables in the oven. When they are cooked, peel the pepper and cut into strips, and scoop out the potato, aubergine and onion flesh, leaving the skins intact.

3. Stuff the vegetables with the rillette and grill in the oven with a little grated onion and grated bread.

4. Mash the peeled sunflower seeds with a little olive oil and strain.

## Presentation:

Pour some of the thickened stock in the bottom of a soup bowl. Trace a circle with the sunflower seed oil and lay the stuffed vegetables on top. To round off, sprinkle with chopped chives and olive oil.

# Roast Vegetables Stuffed with a Rillette of Cock's Combs and Chicken Gizzards

## Ingredients:

50 ml thick chicken stock \ 20 ml egg yolk \ 1 egg white \ 1 pot mole poblano sauce (available from South American shops) \ 250 ml mineral water \ 10 g peeled and deseeded tomato \ 10 g avocado \ 10 g free range chicken breast \ 2.5 g coriander \ 1/3 fish paste (1/2 sheet of gelatine) \ 1 g salt \ 0.5 g black pepper

## Preparation:

1. Add the egg white to the chicken stock and whisk over a very low heat until the egg white curdles without it coming to the boil. When it has curdled, break the film of egg white with a ladle, and recover the stock, straining it through an etamine and a fine mesh chinois.

2. Mix the chicken stock with the egg yolk, add salt and pepper and pour 1 cm into tumblers. Cover with cling film and cook in a bain-marie for 35 minutes at 155° C or in a steam oven for 8 minutes at 100° C.

3. For the mole gelatine:
Strain the mole through a chinois and mix with the water. Heat a fifth of the mixture and add 3/4 of the fish paste, combine with the rest of the mixture and strain once again.

4. Confit the chicken breast in olive oil infused with black pepper for 5 minutes at 80° C.

5. For the chicken salad:
Cut the tomato and the chicken in a brunoise, chop the coriander and dress with olive oil and salt.

## Presentation:

To serve, place a teaspoon of chicken salad on top of the mole gelatine.

# Chicken with Mole Sauce

# Ingredients:

60 g duck liver (foie gras) \ 4 tiger langoustines \ 10 ml olive oil (0.4° acidity) \ 1 g Maldon sea salt

## For the jam:

40 g tomatoes \ 2 g salt \ 1 g sprig of fresh thyme \ 1 g sprig of fresh rosemary \ 0.5 g black pepper \ 2 g sugar

## For the marinade:

200 ml dark beef stock \ 10 g fresh ginger \ 5 g chives \ 1 g Scotch bonnet pepper or 6 drops of Tabasco sauce \ 15 ml lime juice

## Preparation:

### 1. For the jam:

Cut the tomatoes in half and deseed. Place the tomatoes on a baking tray and sprinkle with the herbs, 1 g salt and the black pepper. Confit the tomatoes in the oven for 30 minutes at 165° C. Remove, add the sugar, and return to the oven and cook for a further 20 minutes at the same temperature. Mash and strain.

### 2. For the marinade:

Heat all the ingredients for the marinade apart from the chives to 80° C. Cut the foie into four long pieces and place in the 80° C marinade.

### 3.

Peel the langoustines and just before serving, sear in a non-stick frying pan in 0.4° acidity olive oil and salt.

## Presentation:

Spread a spoonful of tomato jam in the middle of a plate on top of a piece of the drained foie. Lay a langoustine against one end of the foie. Sprinkle with Maldon sea salt.

# Duck Liver Marinade with Tomato Jam and Langoustines

## Ingredients:

1 large potato \ 100 g rabbit kidney \ 50 g boletus mushrooms \ 100 ml beef stock \ 2 red onions \ 20 g black truffles \ 25 ml olive oil (0.4° acidity) \ 10 ml sunflower oil

## Preparation:

1. Slice the potato into rectangular pieces (approximately 4 × 6 cm) in a food slicer at number 15. Lay the slices on top of one another on a piece of greaseproof paper greased with oil and salt, cover with another piece of paper and bake in a 160° C oven for 10 minutes.

2. For the filling:
Cut the kidney into pieces, chop half of the mushrooms into a brunoise and sauté in the olive oil until they are slightly crunchy.

3. Mash the truffle with the sunflower oil and the truffle juice and strain.

4. For the mushroom crisps:
Slice the rest of the mushrooms very thinly lengthways and dry in a 100° C oven for two hours or place in a food dehydrator.

5. Cut a few thin onions rings, coat in flour and fry in hot oil. Reserve. Cut the rest of the onion in a julienne and soften in a pan until you obtain a marmalade.

## Presentation:

Fill the potato with the mushrooms, kidneys and onion marmalade in the form of a cannelloni, glaze with the stock and plate. Trace a line with the truffle emulsion and decorate with the mushroom crisps.

# Potato Crêpe with Rabbit Kidney and Boletus Mushrooms

## Ingredients:

500 g Mona Lisa potatoes \ 1 l single cream \ 150 g fresh or conserved duck liver \ 50 g beluga caviar \ 1/2 glass of thick duck stock \ salt and white pepper

For the preparation of this recipe you should use Mona Lisa potatoes or else Liseta potatoes, both varieties that are especially suitable for making purées and creams.

## Preparation:

1. Peel the potatoes, break them into pieces with a spoon and boil them in plenty of salted water for approximately 10 minutes. Drain the potatoes, reserving the water, wash and mix with the cream. Use a food mixer to achieve a very fine cream, to which you should add 200 ml of the water used for boiling. Allow the mixture to rest, and when it has cooled transfer to the siphon bottle. Charge and allow to rest in the fridge for a few hours.

2. Meanwhile, prepare a terrine with the duck liver, using any one of countless methods. Personally speaking, I prepare it by crumbling the duck liver into small uniform pieces and cooking it on a very low heat while mixing it with my fingers. Once seasoned, leave it in the a tin in the fridge for 8 hours.

## Presentation:

To serve, place a piece of the terrine seared on all sides in a Martini glass. Cover with some caviar and surround with plenty of potato foam. Finally, form a ring of duck stock over the foam.

# Potato Foam with Duck Liver and Caviar

## Ingredients for 4 people:

60 g fillet steak \ 12 g blue cheese \ 20 g foie gras \ black pepper \ 12 ml walnut oil \ 100 ml milk \ 100 ml cream \ 8 g whole green peppercorns \ 7 g stabilizer \ 5 g glucose \ 4 leaves of parsley \ 12 ml concentrated beef stock

### Preparation:

1. Wash the steak and cut it into 2 cm wide strips. Cover each strip in cling film and press into the shape of a tube. Cut into 5 g medallions. Sear on a griddle, season with salt and pepper and serve lukewarm.

2. Cut a 3 g cube of blue cheese.

3. Mix the milk and cream together and heat. Remove from the heat and add the green peppercorns to infuse for 20 minutes. Allow to cool and strain. Reheat half of the mixture adding the glucose and stabilizer and bring to the boil. Turn off the heat and add to the other half of the mixture.

4. Cut a slice of foie gras and caramelize in the sugar with the help of a blowtorch.

### Presentation:

Cut the cylinder into three slices and place in a line. On the one in the centre, place a cube of blue cheese and the fried parsley. On the one on the left, place a little scoop of the green peppercorn cream. On the one on the right, place a slice of caramelized foie gras. Add a splash of concentrated stock and trace a line of walnut oil across them.

Note: You can substitute the pepper cream for a more classic sauce.

# Three
# Fillet Steaks

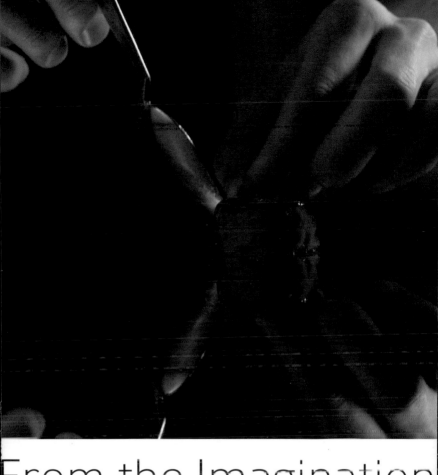

# From the Imagination

## Ingredients:

50 g French bread \ 40 g cured sausage from
Vic \ 1 g salt \ 0.5 g black pepper \ virgin olive
oil \ chervil leaves

### For the foam:

1/4 l tomato juice \ 1.5 sheets of gelatine \ salt
and pepper

## Preparation:

1. Trim the crusts of the bread and freeze.
2. Once frozen, cut the bread into thin slices
using a meat slicer or equivalent.
3. To obtain the bases, place the slices of
bread on a metal baking tray and dry in a
150º C oven for 5 minutes.
4. Season the tomato juice with salt. Heat a
little of the juice to dissolve the soaked
gelatine sheets in, and then add to the rest of
the liquid. Place in the siphon bottle, charge
and leave in the fridge.
5. Finally, cut the cured sausage into fine
slices.

## Presentation:

Place the slices of bread carefully on the
plate and spray with the tomato foam. Next,
add two slices of sausage to each piece of
bread and sprinkle a little olive oil, salt and
pepper over the top. Garnish each canapé
with a small chervil leaf.

# Vic Sausage
# Canapé with
# Tomato Foam

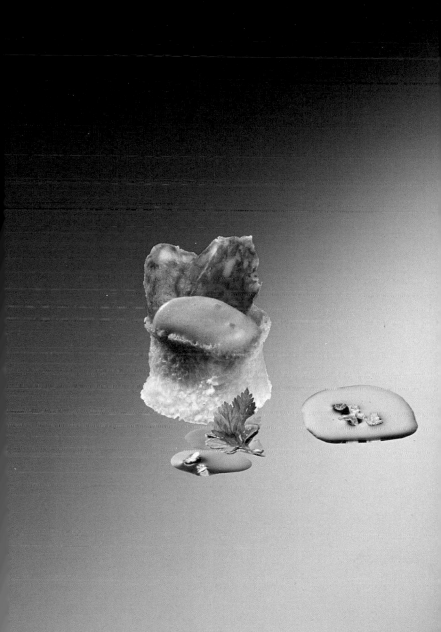

## Ingredients:

French bread \ a scoop of butter for each canapé \ 20 g tin of beluga caviar

### For the caviar foam:

1/2 l of "sea water" (30 g of rock salt dissolved in 1 l of water) \ 3 sheets of gelatine \ 150 g grey mullet eggs

## Preparation:

1. The first thing to do is put the loaf with the ends trimmed into the freezer. Once it is frozen, cut it into thin slices using a meat slicer or equivalent. Place the slices on a metal baking tray and dry in a 150° C oven for 5 minutes.

2. Place the sea water and the grey mullet eggs in a Thermomix. Blend and strain. Heat a little of this mixture and dissolve the sheets of gelatine. Allow the mixture to cool for the gelatine to set. Strain once again and transfer to the siphon bottle, charge and allow to rest. All that is left to do is scoop the butter into little balls and reserve in iced water.

## Presentation:

Carefully take the slices of bread and place a scoop of butter on each one. Next, fill each one with caviar foam, using the siphon without the stem. Finally, carefully place a few caviar eggs on one side with a small knife.

# Caviar and Butter Canapé

## Ingredients:

4 anchovy fillets \ 1 liquidized red pepper \ virgin olive oil \ freshly ground black pepper \ 100 ml garlic infused oil

### For the toast foam:

200 g bread \ 400 ml full fat milk \ 400 ml cream \ salt and freshly ground white pepper

## Preparation:

1. To make the foam, toast the bread until well done. At the same time, mix the cream and the milk together and bring the mixture to the boil. Remove from the heat, add the bread and allow to infuse. After it has cooled down, strain and pour into a siphon bottle.

2. Liquidize the red pepper and add 25 g of sugar. Reduce and emulsify with the garlic infused oil.

3. Fillet the anchovies and place two fillets between two sheets of parchment paper, and then press the fillets lightly with a rolling pin. Roll them around your index finger to achieve the roll.

## Presentation:

Cover the bottom of a soup bowl with olive oil and draw a circle on top with the red pepper paste. Place the rolled anchovy in the middle of the pepper and fill it with the bread foam, topped with a little ground pepper.

# "Tec"
# Anchovies
# with Bread
# Foam and
# Red Pepper
# Reduction

## Ingredients:

500 g cucumber \ 3 sheets of gelatine \ 10 ml teriyaki \ 50 ml water \ 10 g salmon or trout roe

## Preparation:

### 1. For the cucumber foam:

Cut the cucumber, leaving one part peeled and the other unpeeled. Deseed the cucumber, liquidize and strain. Add the gelatine to a quarter of a litre of the cucumber liquid, heat, and then add the rest of the liquid. Use 7 sheets of gelatine per litre. Allow to cool and pour into the siphon bottle. Charge and keep cool.

### 2. For the teriyaki gelatine:

Mix the water and the teriyaki and add 2 sheets of gelatine to part of the liquid. Thicken and transfer to a sauce bottle, keeping cool. Wash the fish roe in "sea water" (30 g salt per litre of water).

## Presentation:

Trace a line of gelatine along one side of the bottom of a small crystal soup bowl, and place the roe on the other. Squirt the foam in between, crowned with a mint leaf.

# Cucumber and Mint Foam with Trout Roe

## Ingredients:
50 ml virgin olive oil \ 4 sprigs of chervil

### For the powdered chilli ice cream:
60 g Basque pickled chillis \ 150 ml water \ 1.5 g salt

### For the potato brunoise:
60 g potato \ 8 g garlic \ 5 g parsley

### For the Roquefort foam:
1 sheet of gelatine \ 60 ml whipped cream \ 40 g Roquefort cheese \ 50 ml milk

## Preparation:

### 1. For the powdered chilli ice cream:
Mash the deseeded chilli with the water and 1 g of salt. Heat part of the liquid to dissolve one sheet of soaked gelatine. Add the rest of the liquid, strain and freeze for two hours.

### 2. For the Roquefort foam:
Heat part of the milk to dissolve the gelatine in and mash the rest with the cream and Roquefort cheese. Combine together, add salt and transfer to the siphon bottle.

### 3. For the potato brunoise:
Cut the potato into very small pieces and mix with half of the garlic and half of the parsley, plus a splash of virgin olive oil. Place in a Roner and confit for 20 minutes at 90° C. After it is confited, add the rest of the crushed garlic and parsley.

## Presentation:
Once the chilli mixture is frozen, process in the Pacojet in portions to obtain powdered ice cream. Place the potato in a bowl and cover with the powdered ice cream.

If you do not have a Pacojet, simply grate the block of ice with a knife to obtain a similar and equally satisfactory result.

# Powdered Chilli Ice Cream with Potato Cubes and Roquefort Cheese Foam

## Ingredients:

12 sea urchin hearts \ 5 ripe tomatoes \ 1 loaf of French bread, sliced \ arbequina extra virgin olive oil \ chervil and black pepper

### For the foam:

1 l cream \ 1 loaf of French bread, sliced \ 350 ml egg white for every 700 ml infused cream

## Preparation:

### 1. For the bread foam:

Toast the bread and infuse in the cream that has just been brought to the boil. Allow to cool and strain through a fine chinois. Add 350 ml egg white for every 700 ml infused cream. Place in the siphon bottle and charge twice. Keep warm in a bain-marie without allowing it to boil.

### 2. For the tomato purée:

Peel and deseed the tomatoes and liquidize them in the Thermomix. Drain slowly through an etamine, pressing against a chinois. When all the water has drained away, lightly emulsify with a little virgin olive oil and season.

## Presentation:

Place three sea urchin hearts on one side of a soup bowl. Beginning from the centre of the plate, start squirting the warm bread foam, making sure the sea urchins are still visible. Spread the tomato purée over the foam, and place a small chervil leaf on top. All that is left is to sprinkle the virgin olive oil over the sea urchin and grind some freshly ground black pepper over the bread foam.

# Sea Urchin au Naturel with Tomato Bread

## Ingredients:

300 g ripe vine tomatoes \ 210 g sugar \ 10 g cheese cream \ 10 g black olive purée \ 100 g fresh bonito \ 25 g mixed salad leaves: savoy cabbage, oak leaf lettuce, chicory \ 100 ml basil infused oil \ 65 g tin of tomato paste

## Preparation:

1. Peel and deseed the tomatoes, add the sugar and place on a low heat until a syrup forms. Drain the tomatoes and reserve the syrup. Add the tomato paste and mash, adding the tomato syrup if necessary. Transfer to a sauce bottle and reserve.

2. Mash the cheese, diluting it with a little milk, strain and transfer to a sauce bottle. It should have the texture of creamy yoghurt.

3. Clean and debone the bonito. Cut into cubes of approximately 25 g.

4. Wash the salad leaves and tear into small pieces. Reserve in iced water.

## Presentation:

Place a drop of tomato jam on the plate and spread it out with a spoon. Trace a line of the cheese cream and a line of the black olive purée over it. Sear the bonito on one side and dress with the basil infused oil. Place the bonito on top of the tomato. Decorate with chervil and freshly ground black pepper.

# Capri Salad

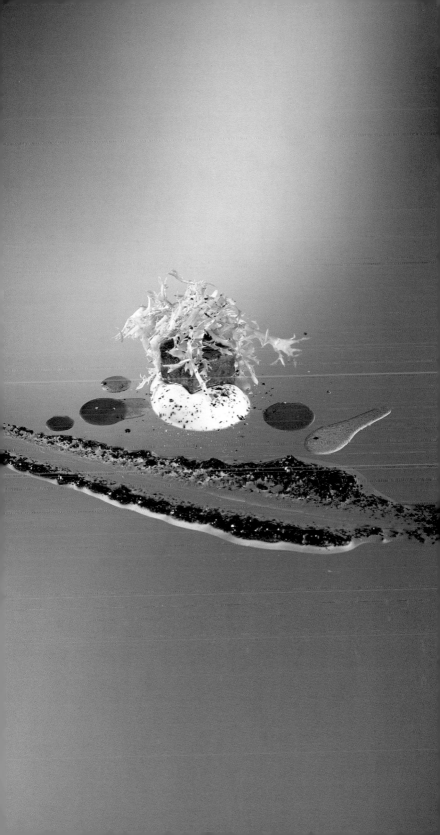

## Ingredients:

200 g white beans (ideally the small Santa Pau type) \ 1 cucumber \ 1 red pepper \ 1 green pepper \ 1 shallot \ 1 tablespoon of finely chopped chives \ olive oil \ salt \ 1 tablespoon of the pulp of black Aragon olives

### For the cod foam:

1/2 kg of desalted cod bones \ 2 tablespoons of garlic infused oil \ 1/2 l single cream

## Preparation:

### 1. For the cod foam:

Lightly fry the cod bones in the garlic infused oil, add the cream and heat, but do not allow it to come to the boil. Remove from the heat. Cover the pan with cling film and allow the mixture to infuse for at least half an hour. Remove the bones, season and transfer to the siphon bottle, charging twice.

2. Bring the beans to the boil, and then change the water. Add an onion and a carrot and simmer for two hours. Mash the olive paste with a little water and emulsify with oil.

### 3. For the salad:

Cut the vegetables into a fine, even dice and mix with the beans and the chopped chives.

## Presentation:

Place a spoonful of the seasoned bean and vegetable mix in an elegant glass. After checking that the foam can flow out of the siphon bottle, fill the glass with the cod foam up to 1 cm below the rim. As a finishing touch, dress the foam with a splash of the black olive emulsion.

# Bean Salad with Black Olive Oil

## Ingredients:

5 g powdered nori seaweed \ 5 ml sesame oil
\ 5 g sesame seeds \ 50 g avocado

For the rice ice slush:
50 g sushi rice \ 0.5 l water \ 4 g garlic \ 2 g
fine grain salt \ 100 ml milk \ 1 bay leaf \ 1
sheet of gelatine (2 g)

For the soy sauce gelatine:
40 ml soy sauce \ 60 ml water \ 1/2 fish paste
or a sheet of gelatine

## Preparation:

1. For the rice ice slush:
Cook the rice with all the other ingredients
apart from the milk for 30 minutes. It should
be overcooked. Strain and add the gelatine to
the rice water. Allow to cool and freeze for
approximately three hours. Remove from the
freezer and scrape with a knife to obtain rice
powder and return to the freezer until
serving.

2. For the soy sauce gelatine:
Mix the soy sauce with the water and heat 1/5
of the liquid to melt the gelatine, and then
add the rest of the liquid. Fill 4 tumblers with
1 cm of soy sauce gelatine and leave in the
fridge for half an hour so the gelatine can set.

3. For the avocado:
Cut into cubes just before serving to avoid it
oxidizing. If you cut it beforehand, cover with
olive oil.

## Presentation:

Place the avocado in the glasses filled with
soy sauce gelatine and sprinkle with sesame
seeds and the powdered nori seaweed. Place
a tablespoon of rice ice slush on top and
finish with a few drops of sesame oil.

# New Sushi

## Ingredients:

120 g smoked salmon \ 50 ml ginger oil (30 ml sunflower oil plus 5 g peeled ginger) \ 50 ml sesame oil \ 50 ml lime juice (juice of 2 limes) \ 30 ml teriyaki sauce

### For the rice ice cream:

250 ml rice water (cooked in the same way as new sushi, replacing the sprig of rosemary with a cinnamon stick) \ 4 egg yolks \ 200 ml cream \ 2 g salt

## Preparation:

### 1. For the rice ice cream:

Cook the rice in the same way as the recipe for new sushi. Add a sheet of gelatine to the rice water and reserve until lukewarm. Whip the custard. Beat the egg yolks with a wooden spoon and transfer to a bain-marie. Slowly add the cream and stir with the spoon until the mixture reaches 80° C and then cook for 15 to 20 minutes. Allow to cool and mix with the rice water. Freeze for three hours, stirring every 15 minutes to avoid it crystallizing. Process in the sorbet maker.

### 2. For the salmon:

Cut into 40 g pieces.

### 3. For the ginger oil:

Confit the ginger in the sunflower oil at 70° C for 45 minutes.

### 4. For the emulsion:

Emulsify the two oils with the lime juice.

## Presentation:

Place the salmon in a soup bowl, and in the centre, make a little opening to support the ball of ice cream. Surround the salmon with the lime emulsion.

# Sushi-Sashimi

Note: As a substitute for the rice ice cream, you can infuse the rice, overcook it and then strain and gelatinize with the rice water. Gelatinize and emulsify with a whisk.

## Ingredients:

For the monkfish gelatine:

1 g salt \ 100 g cleaned monkfish \ 1/2 clove of garlic \ 10 ml olive oil (0.4° acidity) \ 50 ml monkfish stock \ 100 ml cream \ 4 sheets of gelatine

For the ceviche:

1 g salt \ 50 ml tomato juice \ 50 ml orange juice \ 25 ml lemon juice \ 8 drops of Tabasco sauce \ 20 g mango \ 20 g raff tomatoes \ 4 g coriander \ 5 ml virgin olive oil

## Preparation:

1. For the monkfish gelatine:

Clean the monkfish and chop into 5 g cubes, or ask the fishmonger to do this for you. Sauté the garlic until golden and remove from the pan to avoid it burning. Sauté the fish in the same oil on a high heat until it has browned. Remove and infuse in the cream and fish stock, along with the garlic, for an hour. Mash and strain to obtain 250 ml of juice. Dilute 2.5 sheets of gelatine in the juice and strain once again. Transfer to tumblers and gelatinize in the fridge.

2. For the ceviche:

Squeeze the juice from the citrus fruit until you get the required amount of juice and mix with the tomato juice, Tabasco and the salt to obtain 125 ml of liquid. Dissolve 1.5 sheets of gelatine in 25 ml of the ceviche, and then combine with the rest of the liquid. Once the monkfish gelatine has set in the fridge, pour over the ceviche, mix and wait for it to set. Cut the raff tomatoes into a uniform brunoise. Chop the coriander as finely as possible.

## Presentation:

Place the brunoise, dressed with virgin olive oil and salt, on top of the ceviche, and finish by sprinkling with the coriander.

# Monkfish Ceviche

## Ingredients:

1 slice of white sliced bread \ 250 ml arbequina extra virgin olive oil (0.4° acidity) \ 1 g ground black pepper \ thyme flower

### For the cream:

250 ml cream \ 250 ml milk \ 250 g chicken wing meat

### For the chicken stock:

1 kg chicken wings \ 1 leek \ 1 carrot

### For the thyme zabaglione:

2 l cream \ 1 l milk \ 160 ml egg yolks per litre \ 6 sheets of gelatine per litre \ 4 cloves of garlic \ 3 bunches of thyme

## Preparation:

1. Pluck the chicken wings and blanch once. Cover with cold water and just when it comes to the boil turn the heat down to the minimum. Wash and chop the vegetables until you have a mirepoix and add to the pan. Cook for two hours and reserve in the stock. When it is lukewarm, remove the chicken meat from the bones and leave it in the stock.

2. For the chicken cream, mix the cream and milk together and bring to the boil. Add the drained chicken meat and allow to cook slowly for 5 more minutes. Remove from the heat and allow to infuse for 15 minutes. Transfer to the Thermomix and blend until it is a fine cream.

3. For the thyme zabaglione, boil the cream and the milk and remove form the heat. Add the thyme and the cloves of garlic and cover with cling film. Allow to infuse for 15 minutes, strain and place in the 1 litre Thermomix bowl, along with 160 ml egg yolks per litre. Blend for 5 minutes at 80° C at speed 3. Add the gelatine, strain and season. Fill the siphon, charge it and keep cool.

# Cream of Chicken Soup with Thyme Zabaglione

4. Freeze the bread, cut it into small squares and fry in olive oil. When it has turned golden, remove from the oil and drain.

## Presentation:

Spray the thyme foam around the inside of a tumbler. Sprinkle with virgin olive oil and 4 little pieces of toast, followed by some freshly ground black pepper. Decorate with a sprig of thyme. Bring out a jug filled with the hot chicken soup.

# Ingredients for 4 people:

100 g streaky bacon

## For the chestnut soup:

1 kg roast chestnuts \ 750 ml cream \ 750 ml milk \ salt and white pepper

## For the sweet potato purée:

200 g sweet potatoes \ 50 ml water \ salt

## For the barbecue sauce:

100 g pork spare ribs in barbecue marinade \ 50 ml red wine \ salt \ 200 ml water

## For the bacon ice cream:

250 g smoked bacon \ 500 ml milk \ 17 g ice cream stabilizer \ 20 g glucose

## Preparation:

1. Infuse the whole chestnuts in the milk and cream. Heat the mixture and cook very slowly for an hour. Remove from the heat and reserve until cool and cover with cling film.

2. Once cooled, strain and season and serve lukewarm.

3. Roast the sweet potatoes wrapped in aluminium foil for an hour at 180º C.

4. Remove the flesh from the sweet potatoes with a spoon and place in a Thermomix. Add the water, blend, strain and season.

5. Cut the spare ribs into pieces and fry in a little oil in a casserole dish until golden brown. Pour in the wine and reduce. Add the water and allow to cook slowly for half an hour. Strain, season and thicken.

6. Cut the smoked bacon into pieces and lightly fry in its own fat in a casserole dish. Once it has browned, add the milk and the cream and bring to the boil and remove from the heat. Cover with cling film and allow to infuse for 45 minutes.

7. Strain and season the mixture. Boil part of it with the stabilizer, remove from the heat and add the glucose. Allow to rest for 24 hours, freeze and process in the Pacojet.

# Chestnut Soup with Sweet Potatoes, Streaky Bacon, Bacon Ice Cream and Barbecue Sauce

8. Cut the streaky bacon into little cubes and fry in its own fat in a frying pan until golden brown.

## Presentation:

Place the sweet potato purée in the centre of a soup bowl, and pour the lukewarm chestnut soup around it. Encircle the purée with the just fried crispy bacon cubes, and on top of them pour the spare rib sauce. To finish off, place a scoop of ice cream onto the purée.

Note: The bacon ice cream can be substituted by bacon foam or cream.

## Ingredients:

**To confit the truffles:**

60 g summer truffles \ salt \ whole black pepper \ 2 bay leaves \ 400 ml sunflower oil \ 200 ml black truffle oil \ 1 chilli pepper

**For the foie ice cream:**

200 g fresh duck liver \ 15 ml liquid glucose \ 100 ml clear light chicken stock \ 4 egg yolks \ 5 g stabilizer \ grey salt \ chives

## Preparation:

1. Clean the truffles and peel the skin using a microplane grater and reserve. Place in the sunflower oil with salt, black pepper grains, bay leaves and the chilli pepper. Vacuum pack and place in the Roner at 80° C for 30 minutes if the truffles are small, 45 minutes if they are medium sized and one hour if they are large. Keep refrigerated and slice thinly with a mandolin just before serving.

2. For the foie ice cream, add the stabilizer to the cold chicken stock and slowly bring to the boil. Place in the Thermomix and slowly add pieces of foie. While it is blending, add the egg yolks and season. Strain and pour into beakers to freeze. Process in the Pacojet before serving.

3. Mash the truffle shavings with a little truffle oil and sunflower oil until you obtain an emulsion.

4. Chop the chives.

## Presentation:

Lay three fine slices of truffle on a small square plate and spray a little truffle oil over them with the Misto spray and sprinkle a few grains of grey salt. Spoon some of the emulsion around the truffles and place a scoop of the foie ice cream on top.

# Slices of Summer Truffles with Duck Liver Ice Cream

## Ingredients:

4 rounds of toasted ciabatta \ 50 g cream cheese \ 50 g blue cheese \ 100 g marinated chanterelle mushrooms \ 4 leaves of dried spinach \ nutmeg for grating \ salt and pepper \ 6 cloves of garlic \ 3 shallots \ 1/2 red onion \ 1 sprig fresh thyme \ 1 sprig fresh rosemary

### Preparation:

1. Wash the mushrooms and cut them into equal sized halves.

2. Pick the spinach leaves and clean. Fry them in oil.

3. Mash the cream cheese and the blue cheese together, strain and reserve.

4. To prepare the escabeche, lightly fry the garlic, shallots and onion with the herbs, caramelize with a little honey and add the soy sauce and vinegar. When it has reduced, add the stock, and reduce once again and bind. Strain and reserve.

5. Sauté the mushrooms and pour over the escabeche. Cook covered in a 150° C oven for 10 minutes.

### Presentation:

Toast the bread and spread with the cheese paste. Add the escabeche mushrooms and place under the grill. Cover with the spinach crisps and sprinkle over a little salt and nutmeg.

# Blue Cheese, Escabeche Chanterelle Mushrooms with Nutmeg and Spinach Crisps on Toasted Ciabatta

## Ingredients

60 g Williams pears \ 60 g duck prosciutto \
8 g sugar \ 15 ml aged Cabernet Sauvignon
vinegar \ 15 ml Poire Williams liqueur \ 15 g
parsley leaves \ 5 g garlic \ 10 ml olive oil (0.4°
acidity) \ 4 g sprig thyme \ 1.5 g salt \ 0.5 g
black pepper

## Preparation:

### 1. For the pear:

Cut the pear into four pieces and turn it like a
potato. Heat the sugar in a small non-stick
frying pan, and when it begins to change
colour add the pear. Caramelize and then add
the vinegar and the pear liqueur. Cook for 2
minutes, making sure the pears do not go
soggy in the middle.

### 2. For the duck prosciutto:

Cut the prosciutto very thinly and remove
half of the fat. If you buy it already sliced, you
should also remove the fat.

### 3. For the "picada":

Blanch the garlic three times, starting out
with cold water, and crush with the parsley
leaves. Emulsify the mixture as if you were
making mayonnaise.

## Presentation:

Place the pears in the centre of a small flat
plate with slices of duck prosciutto on top,
laying them over each other (approximately
15 g per person). Encircle everything with a
ring of the "picada". Sprinkle some crystals of
Maldon sea salt over the prosciutto and
garnish with a sprig of thyme.

# Caramelized
# Pear with Duck
# Prosciutto

## Ingredients:

1 Granny Smith apple \ 30 g dried beef \ 20 g cured Manchego cheese

### For the ice cream:

1 l extra virgin olive oil

## Preparation:

### 1. For the ice cream:

Emulsify the oil in a Thermomix by applying three spins of the turbo. Freeze in a Pacojet beaker and process just before serving.

### 2. For the dried beef and the cheese:

Cut them up into very fine slices about 5 cm wide so they fit into a 6 cm baking tin. Cut them just before plating to avoid them drying too much.

### 3. For the apple:

Cut lengthways into 1 cm wide strips, remove the core and sear on a griddle until they turn golden brown.

## Presentation:

Place the apple on a plate inside a cake ring with the slices of cheese and dried beef on top. Remove the ring and add a scoop of ice cream on top. Garnish with chervil.

Note: You can substitute the olive oil ice cream for a mayonnaise foam or just a dash of plain mayonnaise.

# Sautéed Apple with Dried Beef, Manchego Cheese and Olive Oil Ice Cream

## Ingredients:

1 Mona Lisa potato \ 500 ml olive oil (0.4° acidity) \ 100 ml meat juices \ Maldon sea salt \ 2 egg yolks

### For the brandade:

200 g deboned and desalted salt cod \ 150 ml cream \ 300 ml Hojiblanca extra virgin olive oil (1° acidity)

### For the "picada":

20 g raw almonds \ 20 g hazelnuts \ 1 clove of garlic \ 50 g parsley \ 2 slices of bread \ 100 ml olive oil (0.4° acidity) \ salt

## Preparation:

1. For the cod brandade:

Fry the peeled and blanched garlic cloves in olive oil until golden. Heat the cream in a pan and infuse the cod and the fried garlic in it. Allow to rest and blend in the Thermomix, binding it with the oil used for frying the garlic in and a little white truffle oil. When it forms a homogenous cream, remove from the Thermomix, strain and season with a little salt.

2. For the potato confit:

Form cylinders with a potato corer and line them up on a chopping board. Trim them so they are all straight and the same height. Fry them gently in a casserole dish at about 80° C in 0.4° olive oil and some salt for 30-40 minutes. When cooked, reserve them in the oil at room temperature.

3. Thicken the meat juices.

4. Finely slice the black truffle with a mandolin and then cut in a julienne for a garnish.

# Potato Confit with Salt Cod Brandade and Black Truffles

5. Beat the egg yolks a little and add the oil in a thin continuous drizzle, season and place in the sauce bottle to trace a line around the plate.

6. Fry the almonds and the hazelnuts in the same oil used for the garlic, then add the

parsley and finally the bread. Blend in the Thermomix and emulsify with part of the oil used for frying (if it has not burnt) plus virgin olive oil. Add salt and strain.

## Presentation:

Place a spoonful of meat stock in a soup bowl. On top, place three potatoes stuffed with the cod, having previously heated them in the oven and grilled them in the Salamander. Encircle the sauce with a fine line of the "picada". Sprinkle a little of the just sliced truffle shavings over the potatoes.

# Sweet Sugar

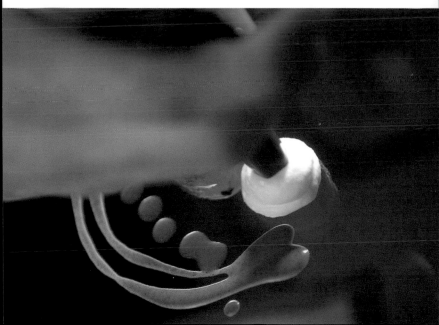

## Ingredients:

1 Greek yoghurt in a sauce bottle \ ground cumin \ 100 g fresh raspberries \ 5 g Maldon sea salt

### For the carrot roll:

250 g carrots \ 150 ml water \ 100 ml T.P.T. (syrup)

### For the pistachio praline:

50 g shelled and peeled pistachio nuts \ 20 ml T.P.T.

### For the carrot soup:

2 carrots

## Preparation:

1. Peel a large, straight carrot, and square off. Cut in half lengthways and cut it lengthways into thin slices with a mandolin. Boil the water and syrup and blanch the carrot slices, leaving them al dente, and allow to cool. Roll them into tubes, to be filled with yoghurt.

2. For the praline, put the pistachio nuts in the Thermomix and add the T.P.T. syrup. Heat until you obtain a liquid of the required texture, strain and pour into a sauce bottle.

3. For the carrot soup, liquidize and keep cool.

## Presentation:

Form a circle with the pistachio emulsion in a crystal soup bowl. Place the equal sized, straight carrot rolls in the middle and fill with the yoghurt. Grate a little lime over the top and sprinkle with cumin. Between each carrot roll, place a raspberry split down the middle and sprinkle with Maldon salt. Serve the carrot soup separately in a jug.

# Carrots with Yoghurt, Pistachios and Cumin

Note: If you do not want to prepare the cumin caramel you can just sprinkle a little powdered cumin over the yoghurt.

## Ingredients for 4 people:

For the white chocolate brownie:
250 g butter \ 140 g white chocolate \ 200 ml egg \ 250 g sugar \ 120 g flour

For the crème caramel ice cream:
300 ml milk \ 200 ml cream \ 100 ml egg yolks \ 35 ml liquid glucose

For the Afuega'l pitu cream:
240 g Afuega'l pitu paprika cheese \ 120 g sugar \ 200 ml eggs \ 80 g butter

For the neutral caramel:
100 g fondant \ 50 ml liquid glucose \ 50 g isomalt at 156° C

For the caramelized apples:
30 g butter \ 1 Reineta apple \ 1 tablespoon water

For the caramel sauce:
100 ml water \ 100 g sugar \ 50 ml liquid glucose

# White Chocolate Brownie with Caramelized Apple, Afuega'l Pitu Cream and Crème Caramel Ice Cream

# Preparation:

## 1. For the brownie:

Whisk the eggs with the sugar. Separately, melt the butter with the chocolate and then add to the egg mixture. Sieve the flour and add to the mixture, kneading slowly with your hands. Place in a 2 cm deep baking tin, greased with butter and flour. Bake in a 180° C oven for 25 minutes on a baking tray covered with greaseproof paper.

## 2. For the ice cream:

Mix all the ingredients apart from the egg yolks and brink to the boil. Turn down the heat, add the egg yolks and keep on a low heat until the cream binds, making sure it does not go above 80° C. Freeze and process in the Pacojet or the sorbet maker, making sure it does not freeze again.

## 3. For the cream:

Cut the cheese in pieces and place in a bowl with the eggs and sugar. Heat in a bain-marie, stirring with a wooden spoon until it forms a homogenous mass. Take off the heat and add cubes of the butter. Stir vigorously to mix and then allow to rest in the fridge.

## 4. For the caramel:

Spread out the caramel with a rolling pin between two pieces of greaseproof paper. Heat in the oven until it becomes malleable again.

## 5. For the apple:

Peel the Reineta apple and scoop out little balls. Reserve in water and lemon juice. Add the sugar and a spoonful of water to a frying pan and allow it to turn golden without burning. Add the butter and the apple and sauté.

## 6. For the caramel sauce:

Place the sugar and half of the water in a pan and allow it to colour without burning. Pour in the rest of the water to halt the cooking process, dissolve the caramel remaining at the bottom of the pan in the liquid and add the glucose.

# White Chocolate Brownie with Caramelized Apple, Afuega'l Pitu Cream and Crème Caramel Ice Cream

## Presentation:

Cut a circle with a 5 cm diameter from the brownie and cut in half. Add sugar to one half and caramelize with a heated spatula. Place the Afuega'l pitu cream between the two slices and push them together. Transfer to plate and place a little pile of the apple and a scoop of ice cream next to it, and the neutral caramel sheet between them. Top with the caramel sauce.

Note: If you do not want to make your own caramel, you can buy the neutral caramel (pure sugar) and spread it out as indicated in the recipe.

## Ingredients:

For the milk chocolate ice cream:
500 ml cream \ 500 ml milk \ 400 g milk
chocolate \ 8 egg yolks \ 35 g stabilizer

For the semi-liquid black chocolate:
400 g dark cooking chocolate (70 % cocoa) \
400 g butter, melted \ 560 ml egg yolk \ 160 g
sugar \ 4 egg whites

For the chocolate sauce:
160 ml water \ 50 g butter \ 30 g cocoa
powder \ 40 g sugar \ 60 g cooking chocolate
(70 % cocoa)

For the chocolate roll:
100 g dark cooking chocolate (70% cocoa) \
50 g caramelized almonds

For the orange Dentel biscuit:
200 g butter \ 400 g icing sugar \ 90 g flour \
180 ml orange juice \ 100 ml Grand Marnier

## Preparation:

1. For the milk chocolate ice cream:
Heat the cream, milk and stabilizer together
to 80° C.

Pour over the melted chocolate, mix to form
an even mass and add the egg yolks.

Blend the mixture in a Thermomix for 5
minutes at 80° C.

Strain and allow to stabilize in the fridge for
24 hours.

Freeze in a Pacojet beaker and process in the
Pacojet.

2. For the semi-liquid black chocolate:
Melt the chocolate in the microwave, and
melt in the butter to form an even mixture.

Whisk the eggs and the sugar in a bain-marie
until they reach three times their initial
volume.

Combine the two mixtures together slowly to
avoid them curdling. Add the lightly beaten
egg yolks, mixing slowly from the bottom of

## Super
## Macaroon
## Cookies

the bowl without any brusque movements until you have an even mass.

Pour into Flexipan moulds and bake in the oven at 220º C for 4 minutes. Plate ready to be eaten hot.

3. For the chocolate sauce:

Mix the water and the sugar together and heat, and then add the cocoa powder.

Turn off the heat, add the chocolate broken into small pieces and dilute.

Break the butter into small pieces while whisking it with a whisk until it has a shiny, even texture.

4. Place the cream in a siphon bottle and charge for the whipped cream.

5. For the chocolate roll:

Melt the chocolate in the microwave and cut 2 pieces of cling film, one 4 × 15 cm and the other 4 × 6 cm.

Spread the chocolate over the cling film and sprinkle the caramelized almonds on top.

Roll it up and fix with sellotape.

Allow to cool in the fridge, and when it is hardens, cut the sellotape and remove the cling film to leave the chocolate roll.

6. Crush into a powder some Oreo biscuits.

7. For the orange Dentel biscuit:

Mix the butter with the orange juice, the sugar, Grand Marnier and finally the flour.

Spread a little of the paste on a Silpat baking mat and bake in a 180º C oven for 4 minutes.

Turn it over and bake for a further two minutes. Remove from the oven and shape with your hands and allow to cool.

# Super Macaroon Cookies

# Presentation:

Draw a few lines on a plate with the chocolate sauce. Next, add the semi-liquid black chocolate and next to it a scoop of ice cream with the Dentel biscuit on top. Fill the roll with the whipped cream and sprinkle with the Oreo biscuits and the almonds.

## Ingredients:

**For the peach confit:**
1 peach \ one part water to one part 50 % syrup

**For the lemon verbena ice cream:**
1 l milk \ 500 ml cream \ 50 g lemon verbena \ 15 g ice cream stabilizer \ 225 g egg yolks \ 150 ml liquid glucose \ 100 ml 50 % syrup

**For the almond macaroni:**
560 g powdered almonds \ 960 g icing sugar \ 480 ml egg white \ 50 g flour

**For the caramelized coconut:**
100 g grated coconut \ 50 g sugar \ 50 ml water

**For the curry caramel:**
100 g curry powder \ 200 ml liquid glucose \ 1 l water \ 100 ml 50 % syrup

**For the Amaretto gelatine:**
750 ml Amaretto \ 250 ml 50 % syrup \ 5 sheets of gelatine (2 g each)

**For the leek crunchie:**
1 leek \ 100 ml 50 % syrup, watered down

# Peach Confit with Amaretto and Leek Crunchies

## Preparation:

1. For the peach confit:

Peel the peach and scoop out balls with a scoop. Cook in the syrup of half water, half sugar for 10 minutes at 80° C. Reserve in the syrup.

2. For the ice cream:

Heat the cream and the milk. When they come to the boil, add the lemon verbena and allow it to infuse until the mixture cools. Strain and return to the heat with the glucose and stabilizer. Bring to the boil, and then remove from the heat and allow to cool. Add the egg yolks and blend in the Thermomix for 5 minutes at 80° C. Strain and allow to cool, and then process in the Pacojet. Allow to rest for 24 hours and freeze.

3. For the almond macaroni:

Mix all the ingredients and spread them in a Flexipan tin in the shape of small chocolates (2.5 cm diameter). Bake in a 180° C oven for 5 minutes.

4. For the caramelized coconut:

Heat the syrup and mix in the grated coconut. Allow to rest for two hours and drain. Spread out between two pieces of parchment paper and bake in a 90° C oven until it turns slightly yellow.

5. For the curry caramel:

Mix the glucose, syrup and water, and heat to 110° C. Add the curry powder and allow to cool. Strain and pour into a sauce bottle.

6. For the Amaretto gelatine:

Heat the syrup and dilute the soaked sheets of gelatine in it. Add the Amaretto, strain and allow to cool.

# Peach Confit with Amaretto and Leek Crunchies

7. For the leek crunchie:

Peel the outer layers of the leek, cut it in half lengthways and dip in T.P.T. syrup (syrup made from equal amounts of water and sugar). Place on a Silpat baking mat and

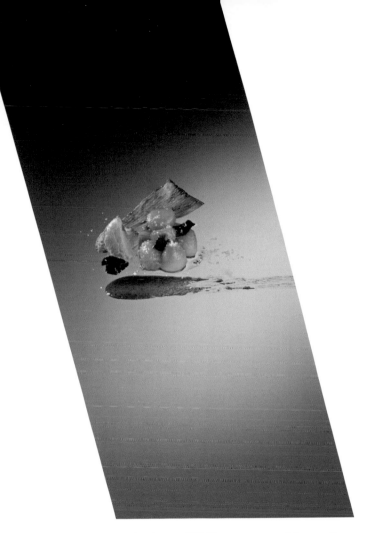

dry in an 80° C oven covered by another
Silpat mat until it has dried out and become
crispy.

## Presentation:

Place a spoonful of caramel curry on a plate
and spread it out with the back of the spoon.
On top, place the peach balls, the broken
pieces of gelatine and the almond macaroni.
Place a scoop of lemon verbena ice cream at
the side, topped with a leek crunchie and
the caramelized coconut.

## Ingredients:

2 oranges \ 100 g slivered almonds, toasted \ 100 ml Grand Marnier

### For the turron foam:
100 ml milk \ 200 g almonds \ 300 ml olive oil (0.4° acidity) \ 80 g sugar

### For the orange custard:
250 ml cream \ 1 orange \ 55 ml egg yolk \ 40 ml orange juice \ 1 sheet of gelatine

### For the crème caramel ice cream:
60 ml full fat milk \ 140 ml cream \ 45 ml egg yolk \ 30 g sugar

### For the orange reduction:
250 ml orange juice \ 25 ml liquid glucose

### For the caramel crystal:
30 g fondant \ 15 ml liquid glucose

### For the sponge cake:
75 g butter \ 55 g sugar \ 1 egg yolk \ 1 egg \ 100 g flour \ 3 g Royal baking powder \ 50 ml egg whites

## Preparation:

### 1. For the turron foam:
Fry the almonds in the oil at 160° C until they turn golden brown, drain on kitchen roll and coat with sugar in a frying pan. Heat the milk until it comes to the boil, add the almonds and allow them to infuse until the milk has cooled. Mash, strain, pass through an etamine and reserve, keeping cool. Place in a siphon bottle and charge.

### 2. For the orange custard:
Peel the oranges with a peeler without removing the white pith. Place the orange peel in the milk in a pan and bring to the boil. Remove from the heat and leave to infuse until it cools and drain. Mix the egg yolks with the orange juice squeezed from the oranges you have already peeled, adding the cream

# Orange Sponge with Crème Caramel Ice Cream and Turron Foam

while whisking. Place in the Thermomix and mash at setting No. 4 at 80° C for 5 minutes. The result should be a fine thick cream. Remove and strain. Place the sheet of gelatine to soak and dissolve it in the cream. Keep cool.

3. For the crème caramel ice cream:

Place the milk and the cream in a pan and heat. Mix the egg yolks with the sugar in a bowl, and slowly pour this mixture into the hot milk, whisking all the while. Heat to 80° C, remove from the heat and strain. When it has cooled down, transfer to the sorbet maker.

4. For the orange reduction:

Put the glucose and the orange juice in a saucepan on low heat and reduce until it becomes a syrup. Remove from the heat and allow to cool. Transfer to a sauce bottle.

5. For the caramel crystal:

Mix the fondant and the glucose and heat steadily to 156° C, remove from the heat and spread onto parchment paper. Once it has cooled, cover with another sheet of parchment paper and place on a baking tray. Reheat in the oven at 110° C until it becomes malleable. Knead with a rolling pin until it forms a thin layer, like fine crystal, as fine as possible. Remove from the heat, allow to cool and store in a dry place at room temperature.

6. For the sponge cake:

Whisk the butter and the sugar with a hand mixer until it whitens and takes on a spongy texture. Mix the egg yolks and the eggs on indirect heat and add to the previous mixture. Combine the flour and the baking powder and add to the mixture. Whisk the egg whites with the sugar until they form soft peaks and add to the mixture. Mix carefully without brusque movements until it becomes a even dough. Place the dough in a cake tin greased with butter and flour and bake at 175° C for 20 minutes. To achieve the best results, the ideal thickness is 3 cm. Allow to cool and remove from the mould.

# Orange Sponge with Crème Caramel Ice Cream and Turron Foam

7. For the caramelized orange segments:

Peel the oranges and remove the white pith. Heat the sugar in a frying pan and when it begins to change colour, add the orange segments. Caramelize for a few seconds and pour over the Grand Marnier to enhance the flavour.

## Presentation:

Cut the sponge into a rectangle and slice open into three pieces, as if it were a sandwich. Place the caramelized orange segments on the first slice, cover with another slice of sponge, followed by the orange cream and the third slice of sponge. Squirt the turron foam next to the sponge. Add a scoop of crème caramel ice cream, topped with the orange reduction and the toasted slivered almonds. Place the sheet of caramel crystal between the ice cream scoop and the turron foam.

Note: You can substitute the crème caramel ice cream for vanilla.
You can buy the caramel in a shop and spread it as indicated.

## Ingredients:

3 slices of white bread \ 100 g icing sugar

**For the chocolate ice slush:**
500 ml water \ 1.5 leaves of gelatine, soaked \ 200 g cocoa powder (22 % cocoa)

**For the liquid cocoa nougat:**
60 g cocoa powder \ 20 g glucose \ 120 ml syrup

**For the chocolate sorbet:**
15 g sugar \ 10 g glucose \ 180 ml water \ 10 g cocoa powder \ 5 g stabilizer \ 60 g Guaranda cooking chocolate

**For the chocolate sauce:**
80 ml water \ 25 g butter \ 15 g cocoa \ 20 g sugar \ 30 g Guaranda cooking chocolate

## Preparation:

**1. For the bread cups:**
Slice the frozen bread very finely and place each piece in cylindrical tins in the shape of a cup. Bake in a 180º C oven for 3 minutes.

**2. For the chocolate ice slush:**
Mix the cocoa and the water and bring to the boil. Heat the syrup and add the gelatine, and combine with the liquid cocoa. Pour into Tupperware containers and freeze.

**3. For the liquid cocoa nougat:**
Boil the glucose and the syrup and add the cocoa powder. Blend in the Thermomix and strain. Allow to cool and transfer to a pastry bag. Spread out between two sheets of parchment paper and bake in the oven at 150º C for 3 minutes. Remove, and before it cools down shape into nests with your hands.

**4. For the chocolate sorbet:**
Put the sugar, glucose, water, stabilizer and cocoa powder in a pan and bring to the boil. When the mixture is lukewarm, add the melted chocolate. Allow to rest for 24 hours and process in the sorbet maker.

# Bread with Chocolate and Sugar

### 5. For the chocolate sauce:

Melt the chocolate. Heat the water, cocoa and sugar. When the mixture has boiled, transfer to the Thermomix followed by the chocolate and the butter. Process for two minutes, strain and allow to cool.

### Presentation:

Pour some chocolate sauce in the bottom of a plate. Fill the bread cups with the ice slush and place in the centre of the plate. Place a scoop of ice cream between the cups. Add some caramel crystals between the ice cream and the bread, and on top the liquid nougat. Finish off with a sprinkle of icing sugar.

## Ingredients:

**For the apple gelatine:**
1 kg of Granny Smith apples \ 5 sheets of gelatine, soaked

**For the fennel sorbet:**
2 fennel bulbs (300 g) \ 1 bunch of dill (100 g) \ 1 l water \ 50 ml syrup \ 100 ml liquid glucose \ 12.5 g sorbet stabilizer \ 5 g fennel essence

**For the yoghurt caramel:**
25 g fondant \ 13 ml liquid glucose \ 5 g yoghurt powder

**For the fruit:**
1 pink grapefruit \ 1 yellow grapefruit \ 1 orange \ 1 lemon \ 1 lime \ 1 carambola (starfruit) \ 4 fresh lychees \ 2 passion fruit \ 1 pitahaya \ 100 g kumquats \ 1 small punnet of redcurrants

**For the pomegranate reduction:**
10 pomegranates \ 20 ml liquid glucose

## Preparation:

**1. For the fruit:**
Cut the passion fruit in half and remove all the seeds and cut the kumquat into very thin slices. Cut the rest of the fruit into small cubes.

**2. For the apple gelatine:**
Remove the apple core and cut into pieces. Blanch for 3 minutes, allow to cool and liquidize. Strain and pass through an etamine. We warm up a little bit of the apple water and we add the gelatine leaves. We mix it with the rest of the apple water and we let it cool in the refrigerator for two hours.

**3. For the fennel sorbet:**
Chop the fennel bulbs and place in a pan of boiling water along with the dill. Allow to simmer for 30 minutes. Mash and strain through a fine colander.

# Fennel Sorbet and Apple Gelatine

Take a small amount of the fennel purée and dilute the glucose and the stabilizer in it, and then mix with the rest of the purée. Add the fennel essence and allow to rest for 24 hours. After this time, prepare the sorbet in the sorbet maker.

### 4. For the yoghurt caramel:

Bring the glucose and the fondant to the boil until it reaches a temperature of 150º C. Allow to cool and add the yoghurt powder. Spread the mixture out on a Silpat baking mat and break into pieces with your hands.

### 5. For the pomegranate reduction:

Split the pomegranates in half and remove the seeds. Liquidize the seeds and reduce with the glucose to obtain a caramel.

## Presentation:

Place a little apple gelatine in the bottom of a tumbler or wine glass. Place the diced fruit and the passion fruit seeds on top, followed by a scoop of fennel sorbet and a small piece of yoghurt caramel.

## Ingredients:

400 g roast chestnuts

For the French toast:
10 egg yolks \ 3 eggs \ 15 g cornflour

For the lemon ice cream:
500 ml cream \ 250 ml milk \ 4 egg yolks \ 15 g ice cream stabilizer \ 100 ml liquid glucose \ peel of 5 lemons and the juice of 2 lemons

For the orange and cinnamon foam:
350 ml milk \ 150 ml cream \ 100 ml dark syrup \ 4 egg yolks \ 3 vanilla pods \ 6 cinnamon sticks \ 3 star anise stars \ peel of two oranges

## Preparation:

1. For the French toast:
Beat the three egg yolks and the cornflour with a whisk, place in a baking tin measuring 40 × 80 cm and bake in a 150º C oven for 3 minutes.
Cut into cubes, dip in the milk and fry in the hot sunflower oil and coat in sugar.

2. For the roast chestnuts:
Cook the chestnuts in dark syrup for 20 minutes until they are tender.

3. For the lemon ice cream:
Bring the cream and the milk to the boil along with the lemon peel and add the glucose, the stabilizer and the lemon juice. Strain everything and then add the egg yolks and process in the Thermomix at 80º C for 4 minutes. Allow to rest for 24 hours and process in the sorbet maker.

4. For the orange and cinnamon foam:
Bring the milk, cream, dark syrup, vanilla, cinnamon, star anise and the orange peel to the boil. Strain and allow to cool. Add the eggs and process in the Thermomix at 80º C for 4 minutes. Allow to cool once again and transfer to the siphon bottle and charge.

# Chestnuts and French Toast with Lemon Ice Cream and Orange and Cinnamon Foam

## Presentation:

Place three pieces of French toast on each plate with a chestnut on top and a scoop of ice cream next to them. Spray the orange and cinnamon foam between the chestnuts and the ice cream and over the ice cream.

## Ingredients:

60 ml olive oil (0.4° acidity) \ 100 ml lime juice \ 20 ml 50 % syrup \ 1/2 sheet gelatine \ 1 lime for grating \ 10 g icing sugar \ Maldon sea salt \ 1/2 loaf of French bread \ 20 ml liquid glucose \ 30 g fondant

### Preparation:

1. Freeze the olive oil in a Pacojet beaker, and once frozen, process in the Pacojet.

2. For the lime gelatine, dilute the soaked gelatine in a mixture of lime juice and T.P.T. and heat. Allow to cool and transfer to a soup bowl until it covers the bottom.

3. Freeze the loaf of bread and slice as thinly as possible with a food slicer. Each slice needs to be approximately 7 × 3 cm. Place the slices in baking tins 2 cm wide and 3 cm deep. Allow them to dry out in a 90° C oven, taking the form of a cup.

4. Mix the lime juice and the glucose and heat to 110° C. Turn off the heat and allow to cool.

5. Place the glucose and the fondant in a pan a boil until they reach 158° C. Wait until the mixture stops boiling and spread over greaseproof paper. When it has cooled down a little, cut into squares. Place between two Silpat baking mats and bake in the oven. Roll out with a rolling pin. Once it is thin and has cooled down, shape and sprinkle with grated lime peel.

### Presentation:

Place the bread cup filled with a scoop of olive oil ice cream in the bowl containing the lime gelatine. Lay a sheet of caramel over the ice cream and dust with icing sugar.

Note: You can buy lemon caramel. You can also buy neutral caramel and after heating it and rolling it out, grate the lime peel over it.

# Bread with Oil, Sugar and Lime

## Ingredients:

For the guacamole sauce:
500 g avocado \ 100 g spring onions \ 1/2 lemon \ 1/2 bunch of coriander (20 g) \ 300 ml full fat milk \ fine grain salt \ white pepper

For the goat's cheese sauce:
1 kg log of creamy goat's cheese \ 400 ml cream \ 200 ml milk

For the fresh tomato sauce:
1 kg ripe vine tomatoes \ virgin olive oil \ Maldon sea salt

## Preparation:

1. For the guacamole sauce:
Crush the cleaned onions and add the lemon juice. Allow to rest for 10 minutes, mix with the other ingredients, and then mash, season and strain.

2. For the goat's cheese sauce:
Heat the milk and the cream. Remove from the heat and add the cheese, and allow to infuse for 20 minutes. Mash and strain. Serve with a little ground black pepper and virgin olive oil.

3. For the fresh tomato sauce:
Cut the tomatoes in half and add the oil and the flakes of salt.

4. For the breadsticks:
Prepare the ready-made dough by diluting it with water, kneading and allowing to rest for 12 hours. Spread with a rolling pin and cut into strips with a pasta maker (18 cm long, 1 cm wide and 0.5 cm thick). Sprinkle with flour and bake in a 160º C oven for 10 minutes.

# Breadsticks with Three Sauces

# Step by Step

1. Pluck the
parsley leaves.

2. Blanch in
boiling water and
refresh with ice.

3. Blend with the oil
in a Thermomix.

4. Strain through a
fine colander.

# Parsley Oil

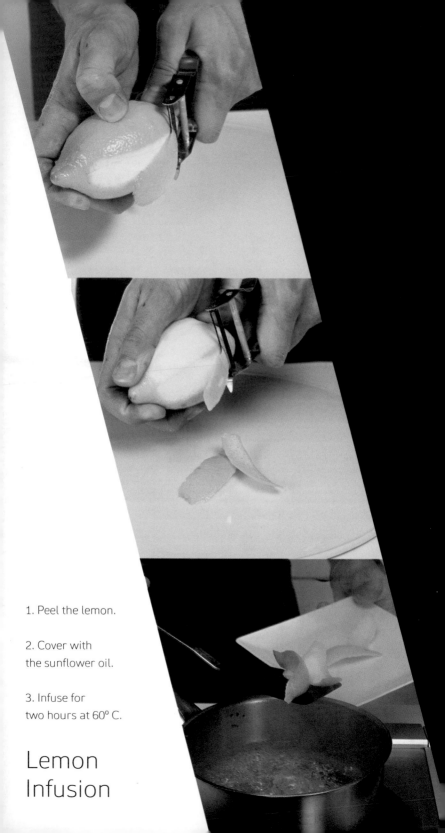

1. Peel the lemon.

2. Cover with
the sunflower oil.

3. Infuse for
two hours at 60º C.

# Lemon
# Infusion

1. Mash the
green pepper.

2. Strain with
a colander.

3. Measure 300 ml
and add 2.3 g agar-agar.

4. Spread out and
allow to cool.

# Green
# Pepper
# Gelatine
# (Agar-Agar)

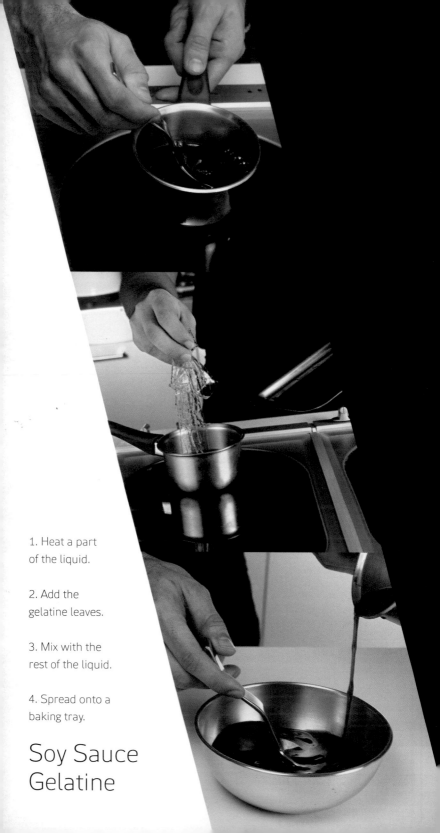

1. Heat a part of the liquid.

2. Add the gelatine leaves.

3. Mix with the rest of the liquid.

4. Spread onto a baking tray.

# Soy Sauce Gelatine

1. Chop
and
sauté the
bacon and
remove
from the fat.

2. Let it infuse
in milk for one
hour.

3. Strain through
a fine colander.

4. Add 300 ml egg
white for every
700 ml of the
remaining liquid.

5. Transfer to the
siphon bottle
and charge. Place
the bottle in the
bain-marie until it curdles.

# Hot
# Bacon
# Foam

1. Toast the bread in the Salamander.

2. Infuse in the cream.

3. Strain through a fine colander.

4. Transfer to the siphon bottle and charge.

5. Allow to cool.

# Bread Foam

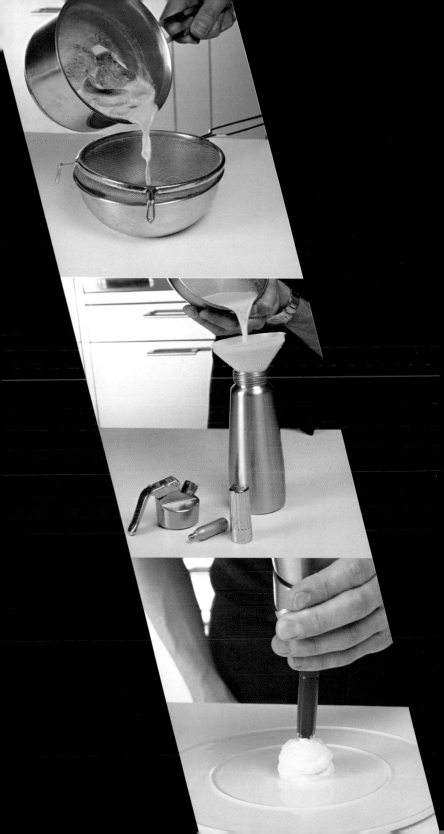

1. Scale.

2. Filet.

3. Place the fillets on top of each other with the loins touching.

4. Cut into squares.

# Sardines

1. Boil the milk.

2. Whisk the egg yolks and milk, heating to 78° C.

3. Mix with the cooking chocolate.

4. Freeze.

# Ice Cream Base

# Glossary of Material

**Blowtorch:** Specially designed for those cooking and baking tasks that require certain precision. It contains a refillable gas cylinder and an adjustable flame. It is perfect for caramelizing, toasting and grilling.

**Charger:** This produces half of the "foam". Each charger contains 8 g of pure $N_2O$ and it is emptied into the siphon bottle once it contains the material that we wish to "air". We normally use one or two for each 1/2 litre or litre, depending on the contents.

**Chinois:** Similar to a strainer, but its conical shape helps channel liquids.

**Colander:** A utensil made out of metal mesh that is used for straining stock, cream, purée, etc., avoiding any impurities passing through.

**Electric saucepan:** Saucepan heated with an electric current and coated in copper, which gives it a high resistance and allows cream based sauces and caramels to be cooked at temperatures of over 160º C without the risk of them burning through contact with the heat.

**Etamine:** This usually consists of a linen cloth, although it can also be a porous bag made out of polypropylene, and is used for separating liquids from solids. It is also used for obtaining a clearer stock.

**Food dehydrator:** This appliance has been created for dehydrating fruit and vegetables while preserving all their vitamins and minerals. You can vary the temperature between 30º C and 65º C. It is normally used to give a crunchy touch to dishes.

**Mandolin:** A small stainless steel utensil that allows us to grate and cut all types of food into slices and strips with ease.

**Microplane Grater:** They were designed for carpentry and perfected for use in the kitchen. They are extremely sharp. There are various models that are used for grating citrus fruit, nuts and spices, cheese and butter.

**Misto Spray:** This reminds us of those typical perfume bottles (vaporizers). They are very useful for dressing and seasoning cleanly and economically. They are also used for giving cocktails the scent of a certain juice or liqueur.

**Pacojet:** A small and extremely powerful machine for making sorbets, that mashes and emulsifies into portions. It is capable of converting puréed frozen fruit at −20° C into a finely ground, perfect sorbet or ice cream.

**Roner:** A digital thermostat developed by Joan Roca that allow us to use a bain-marie with water circulating, ensuring that the temperature is identical throughout the whole recipient. This allow us to control steaming and cooking at low temperatures, from 5° C to 100° C.

**Salamander:** This appliance is like the classic toaster, only a little larger. It is used for finishing the cooking process of certain fish or meat, as a toaster, or to give a final blast of heat to a dish that is almost finished.

**Sauce bottle:** All those plastic bottles that are similar to those found in hot dog stands are termed sauce bottles. They can be filled with oil, sauce, emulsions, purées, etc., and can help us to create lines with greater ease.

**Silpat Baking Mat:** Silicone mat for use in the kitchen, which is totally flexible and easy to handle. It can withstand temperatures of up to 280° C and is useful for rolling dough into slabs or for obtaining crunchies.

**Siphon:** The idea for this came from the classic whipped cream bottles and it can be used for the "famous" foams or sauces, either hot or cold. Both the bottle and head are made of stainless steel, making it easy to use and clean.

**Thermomix:** An easy to handle blender with a thermostat (up to 100° C), controlled speed settings and digital scales. Very useful for obtaining emulsions, creams or purées and perfect for home use, for cooking, making dough, etc. As far as we are concerned, it is one of the most important inventions of the last century. Easy to use and clean.

# Technical Vocabulary

**Agar-agar:** Fresh seaweed that once dried and ground or dissolved in water, stock, etc. allows us to achieve a gelatine that can withstand being heated up to 65° C.

**Blanch:** To leave food in boiling water for a few minutes in order to remove the smell, colour, fat, skin, etc., and then refresh in iced water to impede further cooking.

**Brunoise:** Classic technique of dicing into 1 × 1 mm cubes. It is achieved from a Julienne.

**Caramelize:** The name given to the action of glazing fruit, meat, etc. in sugar that has been transformed into a dark caramel. You can also caramelize simply using sugar and a blowtorch or a heated metal spatula.

**Compote:** Confit fruit and vegetables for at least three hours using sugar, water and spices.

**Concentrated Stock:** The name given to those stocks obtained from boiling bones and pieces of meat or fish for two or more hours.

**Confit:** A method of conserving food. It is also a technique for lightly cooking certain meats and fish, normally in oil or fat at a temperature of not more than 70° C.

**Crunchie:** Name given to the result of preparing meat or fish by drying in the oven or frying to obtain a crunchy texture.

**Crystal:** The name given to a finely rolled caramel made from fondant, glucose and inverted sugar heated to 156° C and then rolled as thinly as possible between greaseproof paper.

**Emulsify:** To give body to oil or liquid with the help of a solid, whether whisking by hand or in a Thermomix.

**Gelatinize:** The action of covering something well with natural gelatine or sheets of gelatine. It can be covered layer by layer (we usually give it three coats) or it can be enveloped in one layer.

**Inverted sugar:** A mixture of glucose and fructose (components of sugar that are used for ice creams and caramels).

**Julienne:** A traditional cut, consisting of sticks approximately 3 cm long by 0.5 cm wide.

**Liquid Nougat:** A mix of glucose, water and solid substances. It is also the name given to the act of moulding glucose. It is obtained by boiling water and glucose, and then mashing it with a solid substance (dehydrated onion, breadcrumbs, chocolate, etc.).

**Mousseline:** Emulsion made from egg yolks and oil.

**Royal:** The name given to a sweet or savoury crème caramel made from curdling a stock simply by using egg yolks that have been steamed or cooked in the bain-marie.

**Sear:** The act of frying or grilling meat until it colours a little.

**T.P.T.:** Syrup made from equal amounts of water and sugar brought to the boil. The initials come from the Spanish expression "Tanto Por Tanto", meaning "like for like".

**Whisk:** To give body to a liquid or a fatty substance, such as cream or egg yolk.